My

Personal

Journal

KeyNotes

BARBOUR
PUBLISHING

© 2005 by Barbour Publishing, Inc.

ISBN 1-59310-648-3

Compiled by Ellen Caughey.

Cover image © AGE Fotostock

Published by Barbour Publishing, Inc., P.O. Box 719, Uhrichsville, Ohio 44683
www.barbourbooks.com

Our mission is to publish and distribute inspirational products offering exceptional value and biblical encouragement to the masses.

Printed in China.
5 4 3 2 1

I can do all things through Christ which strengtheneth me.

PHILIPPIANS 4:13

For God so loved the world, that he gave his only begotten Son,
that whosoever believeth in him should not perish, but have everlasting life.

JOHN 3:16

Thoughts for:

Thou wilt keep him in perfect peace, whose mind is stayed on thee:

because he trusteth in thee.

ISAIAH 26:3

Thoughts for: _____

As far as the east is from the west,

so far hath he removed our transgressions from us.

PSALM 103:12

Thoughts for: _____

Do everything in love.

1 CORINTHIANS 16:14 NIV

Thoughts for: _____

And ye shall know the truth,
and the truth shall make you free.

JOHN 8:32

Thoughts for:

I am a companion of all them that fear thee,
and of them that keep thy precepts.

PSALM 119:63

Thoughts for: _____

Whoever claims to live in him must walk as Jesus did.

1 JOHN 2:6 NIV

Thoughts for:

Let your conversation be without covetousness:
and be content with such things as ye have: for he hath said,
I will never leave thee, nor forsake thee.

HEBREWS 13:5

Thoughts for:

But thou, O Lord, art a shield for me; my glory,
and the lifter up of mine head.

PSALM 3:3

Thoughts for:

But the Lord is faithful, who shall stablish you,
and keep you from evil.

2 Thessalonians 3:3

Thoughts for:

Nor height, nor depth, nor any other creature,

shall be able to separate us from the love of God,

which is in Christ Jesus our Lord.

ROMANS 8:39

Thoughts for:

I can do all things through Christ which strengtheneth me.

PHILIPPIANS 4:13

Thoughts for: _____

Therefore if any man be in Christ, he is a new creature: old things are passed away; behold, all things are become new.

2 CORINTHIANS 5:17

Thoughts for: _____

He restoreth my soul:

he leadeth me in the paths of righteousness for his name's sake.

PSALM 23:3

Thoughts for: _____

What shall we then say to these things?
If God be for us, who can be against us?

ROMANS 8:31

Thoughts for: _____

The eternal God is thy refuge,
and underneath are the everlasting arms.

DEUTERONOMY 33:27

Thoughts for:

And let us not be weary in well doing:

for in due season we shall reap,

if we faint not.

GALATIANS 6:9

Thoughts for: _____

One thing have I desired of the Lord, that will I seek after:
that I may dwell in the house of the Lord all the days of my life,
to behold the beauty of the Lord, and to inquire in his temple.

PSALM 27:4

Thoughts for:

"For I know the plans I have for you," declares the LORD.

"plans to prosper you and not to harm you,

plans to give you hope and a future."

JEREMIAH 29:11 NIV

Thoughts for:

For by grace are ye saved through faith: and that not of yourselves:
it is the gift of God: not of works, lest any man should boast.

EPHESIANS 2:8–9

Thoughts for:

Commit thy works unto the LORD,
and thy thoughts shall be established.

PROVERBS 16:3

Thoughts for: _____

Ye are the light of the world.
A city that is set on an hill cannot be hid.

MATTHEW 5:14

Thoughts for:

For since the beginning of the world men have not heard, nor perceived by the ear,
neither hath the eye seen, O God, beside thee,
what he hath prepared for him that waiteth for him.

ISAIAH 64:4

Thoughts for: _____

A father of the fatherless,

and a judge of the widows, is God in his holy habitation.

PSALM 68:5

Thoughts for:

Who can find a virtuous woman?
for her price is far above rubies.

PROVERBS 31:10

Thoughts for:

Blessed is every one that feareth the LORD;
that walketh in his ways.

PSALM 128:1

Thoughts for:

Honour thy father and thy mother:
that thy days may be long upon the land
which the LORD thy God giveth thee.

EXODUS 20:12

Thoughts for:

Faithful is he that calleth you,
who also will do it.

1 THESSALONIANS 5:24

Thoughts for:

Cast thy burden upon the LORD, and he shall sustain thee:
he shall never suffer the righteous to be moved.

PSALM 55:22

Thoughts for: _____

Prove all things: hold fast that which is good.
Abstain from all appearance of evil.

1 THESSALONIANS 5:21–22

Thoughts for:

The Lord is not slack concerning his promise, as some men count slackness;
but is longsuffering to us-ward, not willing that any should perish,
but that all should come to repentance.

2 PETER 3:9

Thoughts for:

And thine ears shall hear a word behind thee, saying,

This is the way, walk ye in it: when ye turn to the right hand,

and when ye turn to the left.

ISAIAH 30:21

Thoughts for: _____

And he arose, and rebuked the wind, and said unto the sea,
Peace, be still. And the wind ceased, and there was a great calm.

MARK 4:39

Thoughts for: _____

Ye are the salt of the earth: but if the salt have lost his savour,
wherewith shall it be salted?

MATTHEW 5:13

Thoughts for:

Verily I say unto you,

Inasmuch as ye have done it unto one of the least of these my brethren,

ye have done it unto me.

MATTHEW 25:40

Thoughts for:

Let all bitterness, and wrath, and anger, and clamour, and evil speaking, be put away from you, with all malice.

EPHESIANS 4:31

Thoughts for: _____

And be ye kind one to another, tenderhearted, forgiving one another,
even as God for Christ's sake hath forgiven you.

EPHESIANS 4:32

Thoughts for: _____

For where your treasure is,
there will your heart be also.

MATTHEW 6:21

Thoughts for:

For whoso findeth me findeth life,
and shall obtain favour of the LORD.

PROVERBS 8:35

Thoughts for:

Let this mind be in you,
which was also in Christ Jesus.

PHILIPPIANS 2:5

Thoughts for: _____

And the world passeth away, and the lust thereof:
but he that doeth the will of God abideth for ever.

1 JOHN 2:17

Thoughts for: _____

Knowledge puffs up, but love builds up.

1 CORINTHIANS 8:1 NIV

Thoughts for:

It is a good thing to give thanks unto the LORD,

and to sing praises unto thy name,

O most High.

PSALM 92:1

Thoughts for:

The blind men came to him: and Jesus saith unto them,
Believe ye that I am able to do this?
They said unto him, Yea, Lord.

MATTHEW 9:28

Thoughts for: _____

Now faith is the substance of things hoped for,

the evidence of things not seen.

HEBREWS 11:1

Thoughts for:

I wait for the LORD,
my soul doth wait, and in his word do I hope.

PSALM 130:5

Thoughts for:

*There hath no temptation taken you
but such as is common to man.*

1 CORINTHIANS 10:13

Thoughts for: _____

Put on the full armor of God so that you can take your stand against the devil's schemes.

EPHESIANS 6:11 NIV

Thoughts for:

Therefore take no thought, saying, What shall we eat?
or, What shall we drink?
or, Wherewithal shall we be clothed?

MATTHEW 6:31

Thoughts for: _____

Let us lay aside every weight, and the sin which doth so easily beset us,

and let us run with patience the race that is set before us.

HEBREWS 12:1

Thoughts for:

Every good gift and every perfect gift is from above.

JAMES 1:17

Thoughts for: _____

That at the name of Jesus every knee should bow,

of things in heaven, and things in earth, and things under the earth.

PHILIPPIANS 2:10

Thoughts for:

Jesus saith unto her, Mary.
She turned herself, and saith unto him,
Rabboni; which is to say, Master.

JOHN 20:16

Thoughts for:

Ye have not chosen me,
but I have chosen you.

JOHN 15:16

Thoughts for: _____

Jesus said unto him,
If thou canst believe, all things are possible
to him that believeth.

MARK 9:23

Thoughts for: _____